# *A Career As An Independent Consultant*

IS THIS A GOOD IDEA? AND HOW WILL I WIN?

*Robert Kennedy*

Copyright © 2014 Robert Kennedy

All rights reserved.
Original and modified cover art by NaCDS and CoverDesignStudio.com

ISBN: 1495255921
ISBN 13: 9781495255922

# FORWARD

Many people have come to realize that the chances of living the American dream (two cars, big house, club membership, exotic vacations, fulfilling retirement, etc.) while working for a company are relatively small and the process is capricious at best.

Independent consulting is an option for attaining the dream and this book is aimed at helping the reader decide if independent consulting is right for him/her and provides the reader with "how to do it" and "how to win" ideas I learned while I was an independent for over 30 years.

In some ways this book is a memoir and is written in a conversational format rather than a textbook. The reader will note that the expression "the rule of thumb is" is used frequently in the book because there are exceptions to virtually every point I make in the book. Every independent consulting experience/career will be unique.

# TABLE OF CONTENTS

| | |
|---|---|
| Introduction | vii |
| Chapter 1 - The Advantages/Disadvantages of Being An Indy | 1 |
| Chapter 2 - Is Being an Indy Right For You? | 7 |
| Chapter 3 - How to Get Started as an Indy | 19 |
| Chapter 4 - The Three Types of Indies | 27 |
| Chapter 5 - How To "Drum Up" Business | 31 |
| Chapter 6 - What are the Indy Traps | 39 |
| Chapter 7 - Staying Alive! | 47 |
| Chapter 8 - How to Prepare Winning Proposals | 61 |
| The Wrap Up | 75 |

# INTRODUCTION

**Who Am I and Why Did I Write This Book**

I am a very rare cat. I was an independent management and marketing consultant for over 30 years.

The reality is that a very tiny fraction of people who make a start at being an independent consultant last more than a year or two or make more than $200,000 a year over the life of their brief career.

I didn't get fabulously wealthy but I made about as much money as a senior corporate executive and because of the tax laws that favor small businesses I kept more than they did. Also, I didn't live my life attending boring meetings, daily kissing the butts of superiors or putting up with company political games. I usually finished work by 2 p.m. every day so I had time to enjoy my family and hobbies. I lived in the location of my choice without the fear of transfer or of being fired on some whim.

I retired at age 58 not because I didn't enjoy the work but just wore out from the travel requirements and the harsh demands of managing clients.

I am smart but not a genius and although I have an MBA, it isn't from the Harvard Business School. But I had just enough talent and I was willing to learn how to succeed. I was flexible enough to "do what it takes" to stay in business.

This book is a compilation of everything I learned during my 30 years of independent consulting. At various times in my career, I was employed as a sub-contractor for a variety of other consulting firms and learned the good, the bad and the ugly from each. I learned the most from my own mistakes – and there were plenty – but never the same mistake twice.

Here are a few things you need to know before you read this book:
- I have never read any book about consulting so I am uncertain if any other book will give the reader similar or identical lessons I am presenting in this book.
- It is aimed at people who are considering a career as a long term independent consultant and not for people who are interested in a career at a larger consulting firm or plan to be an independent consultant for a short period of time while they look for employment at a client company.
- For reading ease I refer to a long term independent consultant as an "Indy" and the nickname for Indiana Jones is seemingly appropriate for the type of people who succeed as long term independent consultants.
- I have changed a few stories and exaggerated a few examples to make a point or to make sure you, the reader, really pay attention to the point being made.
- I am not a lawyer or an accountant – so I am not offering any legal or accounting advice. In these matters always utilize the services of people you know and respect.

I hope to help readers make the right decision to become – or not become – an Indy and this book will give them every opportunity to succeed if they choose to enter the profession.

# Chapter 1
# THE ADVANTAGES/DISADVANTAGES OF BEING AN INDY

### Advantages of being an Indy

For me, the greatest benefit of being an Indy was the general sense of freedom I had, but there are a number of very specific benefits of being an Indy:

1. Financial

    The financial rewards for Indies can be substantial if you are successful. To a large degree you will earn about as much as you really, truly want and are willing to make the sacrifices required. As a very general rule of thumb figure you will earn about as much as a midsized company vice president. Also, the Indy should be able to keep more of what he/she earns than a corporate person.

    - As a business sole proprietor you will enjoy a number of tax advantages over company stiffs
    - There are also no "keeping up with the Jones" expenses such as fine clothes, luxury car ownership, club membership, etc.
    - You get to keep all frequent flyer and hotel frequent stay-er points
    
    There is always the chance of "hitting the ball out of the park" because as an independent person, you might come upon some very golden business/investment opportunities.

2. Time flexibility
   This is a big deal. I worked when I felt like it and didn't work when I didn't feel like it. I am very productive in the morning and progressively less productive in the afternoon. I generally worked from 8am to about 2pm every week day. This was no 9 to 5 hours "just to be there" job for me. Depending on my work load I would work on weekends and holidays. I could always attend parent teacher conferences and my child's sports events.

3. Around home
   I worked from home so I was an active participant in the raising of my child and not some distant parental figure. Also, I was able to accomplish "honey-do" work around the house and garden when I needed a writing break or had serious down time.

4. Work accomplishment satisfaction
   When you work for the Man, successes have many parents – but as an Indy you will feel a real sense of satisfaction of completing a piece of work. **There is a very real Zen feeling when you solve a case or provide a client with a meaningful module.**

5. No office negatives – Let me count the ways!
   This was a biggy for me as I just never did fit into the corporate environment.
   - No boss – enough said!
   - No company politics, back stabbing, etc.
   - No worthless meetings – affirmative action, sexual harassment, fire policy – the list is endless and in those meetings you can just see your life slipping away. They are like prison, but worse.
   - No "being nice" all day, every day.
   - No employee problems – you have no employees.
   - No good looking young honeys/studs to tempt you.
   - No fear of sexual harassment lawsuits or firings.

- No fear of being fired!
- No fear of being transferred – say to East Jesus, North Dakota.
- No unfair evaluations – when I worked for the Man, I was always misjudged as being too smart or not smart enough or too soft or too hardnosed.
- You can live where you want to live and not where the company is located.
- You make your own destiny and you are not dependent upon how lucky you might be in the corporate environment to "grab the brass ring." Face it: as the pyramid dramatically narrows near the top, luck plays a big role in who actually makes it to the top.

6. Here is a tough one to describe: Freedom from socio/economic class and the ability to form your own persona.

    Perhaps my example will help: I grew up in an upper middle class environment, became an Army Officer, went to B School and then became a "suit" working for the Man. I was the classic suit mocked in popular movies. After I was an Indy for a while I thought of myself as a "working man." **I had truly become my own man**. This is a big deal that you may not appreciate until it happens to you.

7. Limited to no capital requirements compared to other entrepreneurial pursuits

    Think no franchising fee, long term leases or the purchasing of equipment. If you fail as an Indy you will only lose income and time but unless you are very foolish, you probably won't go bankrupt.

8. The thrill of the hunt. I always felt I was in harmony with our ancestor hunter/gatherers. Human beings are naturally predators. If you like participating in sports, you will love being an Indy.

## Disadvantages of being an Indy

There are a number of disadvantages of being an Indy but most of them can be mitigated to one degree or another:

1. Low probabilities of success

Very few people possess all of the qualifications to be an Indy. In the next chapter I will tell you about the qualities you will need to succeed and give you tips to help you succeed.

2. Uncertain and variable income

I once went 6 months without any income and there was always the fear and sense that I was only one step away from going out of business. There are advantages and disadvantages of an uncertain and variable income. On the one hand the uncertain income forced me to save more since I never knew if or when I would throw craps and the Indy gig would be over. On the other hand, I was always in fear of financial failure and not being able to provide for my family and I was unable to invest in investments that require a stable income stream, such as real estate. Variable income is very hard on marriages as spouses are whip-sawed between feeling rich and feeling poor.

3. **No respect**!

I think this is the opposite of what most people think when they think about being an Indy. Whenever I told anyone my profession, you could see that they didn't think much of it – compare that with being a corporate VP or a government official. Also at clients' I was treated pretty much as a hired gun – "hide the women and children and get out of town fast once you have shot the bad guy." If you have been a senior executive and become an Indy, this will be a big shock. I knew a guy who was a senior executive at a respected company who was a long time president of his company's trade organization. When he became an Indy he was very surprised by how few of his "buddies" would return his calls.

4. All alone

You will mostly work alone and not have any company and fellow employee support.

5. You actually have to create/produce something.

As an Indy you can't be a Wally in the cartoon Dilbert nor can you be a typical corporate VP or higher who just reviews other people's work and attends meetings.

6. If you are an Indy long enough, you become virtually un-employable with the Man – you have left the career track.

Welcome to your new job as a shoe salesperson at a department store. Use this fact as a motivator to succeed as an Indy.

7. Short career

Thanks to ageism people really don't trust most folks below 35 to be a consulting wizard and they think you are an old fool if you are over 60. They also figure that if you are so smart, why are you still working at 60? As a rule of thumb, the sweet spot age-wise is between 40 and 55.

8. Legal liability

When you work for The Man, The Man covers most of the legal liability and pays and staffs the lawyers. As an Indy you are potentially liable for just about anything including errors and omissions, breach of contract, etc. I found legal liability to be a relatively small risk because I stayed inside the law and more importantly I cultivated a good relationship with a lawyer and consulted with that lawyer about anything I believed would put me in legal jeopardy. Remember, we live in a very litigious society!

9. As a sole proprietor you will pay double social security – once as the employer and once as the employee.

**10. Competition in consulting is incredibly intense – there are no competitive barriers to entry into the profession. Here are just a few of the types of competitors you will encounter:**
- **The Big Guys –** Large consulting firms that suck up most of the money at clients– they are incredibly talented at figuring out how much money a potential client has to spend on consulting and they manage to get it all in many cases.

- **Other service companies** that try to maximize their revenues at clients by expanding into general consulting – think advertising agencies, accounting firms and the like.
- **New little guys** – let's say you have created a sweet niche as an Indy and you are earning about $200k a year – someone or more will hear about your niche and become competitive with you. Your $200k could halve or in fact disappear – there are no competitive barriers to entry in consulting!
- **Other Indies** – Very rare competition, because most "new guys" don't last long.

In Chapter Seven I will tell you how to handle each of these classes of competition.

# Chapter 2
# IS BEING AN INDY RIGHT FOR YOU?

Just about everyone I have ever known in business, at some point in his/her career dreams of being an independent consultant. It seems so easy and the rewards seem so desirable. Most people only dream about it because they are too scared to leave their cages in the zoo, and the few who do try it lack all of the skills required to stay alive as an Indy. The reality is most people who try to become Indies do so because they have been fired from a job or retired before they were ready – rather than have a passion to become an Indy.

The following are essential abilities and skills of being a successful long term Indy:
- Ability to work alone
- Very likable, attractive, "sexy"
- Great presenter
- Write winning proposals
- An expert
- The right mind
- Ability to manage a business
- A supportive spouse or no spouse at all

**Ability to work alone**

This trait/ability is the sine qua non of being an Indy – the key word here is independent. If you are a very social person who needs to be around people, you will not last as an Indy. Many of the Indies I have known are loners who generally interact with people primarily to use them. If you are normally social and mentally healthy, it helps a great deal to have a social network of family, friends and neighbors and pets. When I was single, my cat constituted the central part of my social network!

**Being very likable, attractive, and "sexy"**

This quality is second on the list because it is one of the most important qualities required for Indy success. In this area you cannot just be above average – you must be exceptional.

It was a shock to me as I thought that being an expert was the most important quality. I am sure it will be a shock to you, the reader. I was sort of likable and sort of attractive, but mostly I had to give up close to 50% of my earnings to contractors who had a load of one or more of those attributes. Human beings are social animals first and rational animals second and they are powerfully driven to be liked, flattered, loved, and sexed.

I once worked with a person who the clients could sense when he was in the office – the phone would ring when he was in and fall silent when he was gone. I did all the work and he collected 50%!

Trust me, if you try hard enough, you can be very likable – to some people it comes naturally. For others like me, I had to work very hard at it (and never got very good at it). For starters, read Dale Carnegie's _How to Win Friends and Influence People_ –memorize it, practice it and always use it.

One great way to be loved is over the years mentor/promote/help subordinates when you are in a position of authority. When those people reach the level of hiring a consultant you can call in the favor. I know one Indy who created an entire 20 year Indy career based almost exclusively on just one person he had mentored fifteen years earlier.

Be the ego ideal of your potential clients – that is, appear to be the same as they are in terms of appearance, culture, interests, language/idioms/jargon, intellect, education, and family life. The guy I mentioned above hated professional sports but he read the sports page every morning so he could smooze clients about their favorite teams.

Because I came from a professional class background, the Yale degree with the Harvard MBA types liked me the best and gave me a lot of business. Also, they were pretty loose with money and expenses and did not get caught up in the nickels and dimes. I just seemed to resonate with the blue blood types and I could camouflage my difference from these guys fairly easily. Unfortunately there are not many of these types of folks around.

I did so-so with the MBA's who arose from the middle class – there are a lot of these guys out there so my "C" grade with these folks hurt me a great deal. These guys were both attracted to and repelled by my more up-scale image.

I give myself a "C-" in working with the up from the ranks guys. They liked the fact that they had some MBA type guy doing their bidding, but they never identified with me. Ironically, I liked these folks the best, but I am sure they thought I was judging them for their smoking, drinking, ethnic jokes, poor grammar and humble beginnings.

Sex sells! Women like to be flirted and men like to be flirted – forget this and you will regret it. Just stay away from any form of sexual harassment.

I thought it was just men who let sex influence their business decisions – wrong! Several times I was invited to a "business dinner" by a female client who obviously wanted a different kind of business. I lost a major piece of business because I just wouldn't flirt-up female clients or prospective clients.

The good news here is that you can partner up or contract with a contractor who is skilled in dealing with folks who you cannot get to love you.

The bad news is that being loved is about 50% of the success of being an Indy, so I had to essentially pay 50% of my fees to the partners and contractors who could be loved by a specific type of client.

## Become a great presenter

Presentations are a critical area for success – about 20% of the skill required to be a successful Indy. I once heard about an Indy who was a really lousy consultant but who was a great presenter. I am sure there are books on how to make presentations, but here are my specific pointers.

1. Make sure you are actually there for the presentation. This means that if you are flying in to the presentation you arrive the day before – never count on the airlines to get you there the same day – at some time in your career you will seriously rue not following this pointer.

2. Never just electronically ship a presentation – always make a presentation and if possible make the presentation in person rather than via electronic video conferencing.

3. While the best and the brightest in my high school were taking classes such as AP Physics and $2^{nd}$ Year Algebra, I – "not the brightest"- took two years of public speaking classes. If you have never taken a public speaking class – do so! Public speaking skills are critical to most Indy success – it just amounts to learning the skills and practice.

4. Speak with passion – dramatize the content of your presentation and dramatize your commitment to the success of the client company and the individuals in the meeting. It must appear that you care more about the success of the client's business than the client does.

5. Avoid any conditional words such as maybe, perhaps, could/would/should. Always use forceful, positive words – like can/will. Also, never use the passive voice.

6. Look like the ultimate wizard in your field – try to know so much about your topic that you won't be tripped up by a question from the audience – and often some member of the audience will try to trip you up. Secret: early in a presentation, say something that is contrary to conventional wisdom to draw out the "tripper" – and then throw out convincing facts that swamp the tripper. That will quiet any potential trippers and make you look like a wizard. If you bring anyone else to your presentations make sure they say

"amen" to whatever you say and don't say anything that weakens your position as a wizard. If you do not know the answer to a question, say "I don't know, but I will research it and get back to you." Do not try to B.S. your way out – you can die with this tactic.

7. Never lose control of your presentation with too many questions from the audience. Remember that the role of questions from the audience is to:
   - Make you look like a wizard
   - Make your client look good for hiring you
   - Get the audience involved in your presentation
   - Provide insights for you for future assignments.

8. Do not just read your presentation from an overhead. Memorize the first work of a bullet and then speak to the bullet point – your presentation should be about 50% more content than is in the written presentation. The reason you are there in-person is to add depth/context to your report – add short stories to highlight key points.

9. Be perfect with grammar, spelling, math, etc. – use a "schoolmarm" type to edit out any errors – Only one error can force you to lose control of your presentation and destroy your image as a wizard.

**Write winning proposals**

Proposal writing is a critical skill a rookie Indy must master. I have seen beginning Indies flame out very quickly because they could not write a proposal. The last chapter of this book is a detailed description of how to write great proposals.

**An expert**

Perhaps the biggest surprise to people who think about consultants is that they don't need to be experts in a field. Of course, being an expert helps. Essentially the more unique the expertise is and valuable it is to a client, the more important it is to being a successful Indy. If you possess the secret to eternal youth, being an expert is the key to success.

But in most circumstances being an expert is the least important success variable for an Indy. Here are the reasons why:

1. Most expertise in an area becomes obsolete over time. Perhaps you are an expert in the manufacturing of buggy whips – what happens when the car is invented? Also, most Indies start out in a very narrow niche – an area in which larger firms do not have an expertise. As a rule, the narrower the expertise, the more quickly it becomes obsolete.

2. In many situations there is a limited customer base for an expertise – when the Indy has run through those clients, what's next?

3. Your expertise can be ripped off by another consultant. I have seen it happen where an Indy develops a market and then two other Indies enter the market and larger companies enter the market.

4. Experts usually come cheap because they lack the other skills needed to succeed as an Indy. I never had any problem hiring experts at a fairly low price. There are tons of people out there who are between jobs or recently retired (with high quality expertise) where a little money and a little work means a lot to them. The between jobs people can add to their resumes that they were in fact not between jobs but "consulting" after their last job. For the retiree, the money is less important than the feeling they are "still in the game" and have something to do besides playing golf.

5. The keys here are either to know enough about an area that you can make the client believe you are an expert, or have a good enough relationship with a client that they trust you to find and use a credible expert.

   Over the life of my career I was an expert in about five different areas. Several consultants I contracted with fooled a client they were experts when they were not and contracted with me to do the work.

**The right mind**

To succeed as an Indy you need to possess a number of mental/psychological traits

1. Above average intelligence – but not necessarily a genius. For the most part, the smarter you are the greater chance you have of success.

2. More important than just intellectual horsepower is mental flexibility and agility– this was my greatest strength. This is the ability to think around problems and issues in a grid-like manner rather than just being linearly smart.

3. Ability to swallow your ego – you, my friend, will be on the wrong side of the desk and must always defer to the person on the other side of the desk (see the section on ego swallowing later in the book). This is a tough one because on the one hand you need to have a strong enough ego to become an Indy, but on the other hand you need to be able to bury it many times when dealing with clients.

4. The ability to be Machiavellian and shrewd. You have to have the ability to use other people. You need to think of clients as prey and you are the predator.

5. Number four above leads to the necessity of being **able to read people to identify any weaknesses that you can exploit be it vanity, greed, holes in moral character, selfishness, unbridled ambition, etc.**

6. Possess common sense – I know lots of really smart people who don't possess this quality.

7. Be goal and achievement focused – no wishy-washy folks I have known have ever been real Indies.

8. Be very strongly self-motivated to overcome your limitations. I had a fear of flying – guess what – I flew all the time anyway. I made cold calls when I hated rejection. I didn't go on vacation for 17 years. You name it!

9. Possess a work ethic. Most of my regrets, looking back, were that I was too lazy – took the easy way – and my wife calls me a workaholic!

10. Be able to solve cases – deliver the goods. I have known very smart people and "experts" not be able to actually solve the problem the client wanted solved. They could talk about it, think about it, but not actually "do it." I was good at this and it kept me in business.

11. Have a strong moral compass – for me the priorities of my life were, in order:
    - My immediate family – my role as a provider and father figure –for me this was the 92%
    - My extended family – 4%
    - My community 2%
    - My State 1%
    - My Nation 1%
    - The World 0%

As you can see only 4% of my Indy career focus was outside my family. The only clients I would not consult with were, in my mind, morally reprehensible or engaged in illegal activity. For my community I used my consulting skills for the preservation of my neighborhood. For the state and nation, I paid my taxes only as much as the law dictated and I voted for the candidates I thought would screw things up the least.

For you, it might include your religious faith. Whatever your moral compass is, follow it and **"stay on strategy."** For many people with a strong social conscience it helps them "strengthen their backbone" to be better Indies. I have never met any of those kinds of folks, but I am sure they are out there.

12. Be emotionally stable – be able to handle rejection, periods of self-doubt, disappointments and failures.

13. Either have a strong tolerance for stress or be able to manage it. I managed stress with meditation, sports, gardening and the occasional angry outburst at airline gate Nazis, and hotel clerks that walked me at 2 in the morning.

14. Be perceived as possessing strong moral character. That means you are perceived as trustworthy, loyal and "a good citizen." You can laugh at ethnic and sexist jokes but not tell them. The point is that you need to be perceived as serious (gravitas) but not "a stiff."

15. Hate to lose! I hated to lose at sports – often would sit in a locker room for 20 minutes after a big sports loss with my head between my hands – in full sorrow mode. I hated to lose in my Indy business. I like the expression: "Show me a good loser and I will show you a loser." When I retired, I switched from participating in a competitive sport to being a hiker.

## Manage a business

As an Indy you are the business – managing a business includes such tasks as accounting, tax preparation, bill paying, invoicing, legal, equipment purchasing and repair, etc. I did some, my wife did some and I had to pay CPAs and lawyers to do the rest.

## A supportive spouse or no spouse at all

A spouse or significant other is a critical area of success or failure for an Indy – read this section carefully – and don't deny, rationalize, or gloss over any of it.

For the most part it is difficult to be an Indy if you are single and/or living alone. Here are variables.

- Remember you are alone most of the time with no office mates – it can be pretty lonely if you are all by yourself all day. A spouse and or significant other provide real human contact. When I was single my pet helped me a little but later, a spouse really helped. I think if you are a single Indy you should participate in group activities such as a sports team, affinity club, etc. A supportive spouse will help you celebrate your victories and console you in your defeats or rejections – this is a big deal as it helps you through the rough spots.
- If travel is an important part of your business, a supportive spouse/live in is essential – a voice from home, taking care of home business, etc. The key word here is supportive – it takes a special type of spouse for a traveling Indy. We are talking someone who is trustworthy, faithful, cheery, loving, and competent.
- We have talked before of income base from a spouse, but the downside is that a spouse can be wrapped up in his/her career and not supportive of the Indy – and have an excuse not to fully support an Indy.
- The spouse must be able to live with your variable income and not have a spending problem.
- A spouse can also contribute to your business – proofreader, errand runner, travel coordinator, critic (but not too much), business manager, etc.

If you are a single Indy, carefully evaluate any potential spouse to see if he/she is appropriate for an Indy – how is he/she on all the above points? If you currently have a spouse, before you become an Indy, make sure you have the big talk and a fulsome (come to Jesus) agreement from your spouse on the level of support you will need. At the end of the day, for an Indy, you are better off single than to be married to an unsupportive spouse.

When you first begin as an Indy, a working spouse is not a bad idea as the spouse generates income to keep you alive while you ramp up your business. But over time, I believe a working spouse is a big impediment and I have never met a long term Indy with a spouse employed out of the house. Here are some reasons.

- The spouse's income will take some of the edge off your hunger to succeed – "why go 100% and take all the lumps if my spouse is bringing in some good bucks?"
- When you are really successful, your spouse's income will be taxed at the last $ you earn. Try telling a spouse that he/she is really only bringing in about 50% of his/her income. Then you add such things as child care, transportation, clothing, etc. – costs that drive the net down to about 30%.
- If your spouse leaves the house at 7am and returns at 6 pm, he/she will get a little cranky that you played tennis at 3pm – and you are the big money earner.
- To really succeed as an Indy, you will need the unconditional support of your spouse – the home base covered – the kids, the house, the extended family. Which brings up the issue of what kind of spouse an Indy needs to succeed:
    - ✓ Can live with an uncertain and inconsistent income – not easy for someone who came from a family with a steady income.
    - ✓ Can be very, very supportive – can suborn their parochial self interest to the good of the family.

**The bottom line on whether you should become an Indy**

Essentially, you can buy via contracting any of the above success variables. Here are the rule of thumb costs of outsourcing Indy skills for each dollar of consulting fees:

Working alone: $1.00
Being loved: $.50
Great presenter: $.25
Great proposals: $.15
Expert: $.20
Right mind: $1.00
Manage a business: $.15

*You can see that if you go near or over a buck, you have no chance of being an Indy. The reality is that you can survive and prosper if you keep about $.40 on the dollar – the challenge is to get up around $.80 on the dollar.*

Now that I have scared the bejeezus out of you, here is a note of encouragement: **When your entire life depends on your success/survival as an Indy, you will be surprised by all of the hidden skills you possess if you look for them and cultivate them – will wins over skill!**

# Chapter 3
# HOW TO GET STARTED AS AN INDY

1. Moonlight

2. Prepare for your consulting career while you still work for the Man

3. Get fired from your day job

4. Work for a larger consulting firm

5. Convert a "non-job" job into a consulting gig

**Moonlight**

I started consulting by moonlighting from my day job. A friend had sold a small marketing research job and didn't know how to conduct the research, so he called me since he knew in my past life I had been a marketing research manager. I moonlighted for a couple of years until I had built a big enough customer base to quit my day job.

Moonlighting as a starting point has a number of advantages:

1. You keep your regular income while you start your business.

2. You test to see if consulting is right for you before you jump in the deep end.

3. If you are in a boring job, or one that does not fill up the time, the moonlighting work can fill in the empty time and give you a new challenge.

4. The income from moonlighting is like mana – essentially most people live to their day job income or budget to it. Revenue from moonlighting drops right into either savings or is used to purchase the "something I gotta have." Also, most of the moonlighting income can be legally sheltered from taxes.

I believe moonlighting is the best entry into independent consulting and most of the people I have known who have succeeded as independent consultants started by moonlighting.

There are some "look out fors" when moonlighting.
1. Make sure the company you are moonlighting for does not compete with your day job company – a good way to be fired from your day job and is a moral problem. My day job was project management in the biochemical industry and my moonlighting work was industry research performed for companies in the food industry.

2. Don't get caught doing moonlighting work on day job time.

3. If possible receive day job supervisor ok that you are moonlighting.

4. Make sure your work performance in your day job does not deteriorate as you ramp up your moonlighting work.

5. Use vacation days to present your findings to moonlighting clients rather than sick days – essentially fraud.

6. Make sure your moonlighting clients don't know about your day job. As far as they are concerned the moonlighting job is your day job.

7. If you moonlight, there is a risk to being fired from your day job - just so you know.

### Prepare for your consulting career while you still work for the Man

I like this approach but I found that most people who work for the Man do not make the effort to set a base for consulting because they are content working for the Man and don't see that down the road they may be fired or fed up and want to become consultants. Ironically, this should be the best entry into Indy-dom, but sadly, working for the Man turns virtually everyone into a herd animal.

The point is: don't wait to be fired or retired early to establish the base for your Indy career. If you are currently working for the man and have the vision and courage to eventually become an Indy, I suggest the following:

1. Join and speak at industry conventions and associations – on a specific area of expertise – get a reputation as a thinker not just a "good guy."

2. Make strong contacts with other people in your day job industry and area of expertise. Follow up frequently.

3. Actually produce something rather than just review other people's work and attend meetings.

4. Collect strong favors or obligations from other people who could at some future date become a client.

5. Become humble – start checking your ego at the door and behave like the person on the other side of the desk – practice puckering up, because once you become an Indy you go from the butt kissed to the butt kisser.

### Get fired from your day job

Two of the most successful long term independent consultants I have known fit into this category. Essentially they were very smart and capable but didn't fit in with larger organizations. One of the guys got fired for going around the country bad mouthing his boss. At some level they realized that if they failed at consulting they were out of luck. This strategy helps if you also have a large mortgage, three children and a stay-at-home spouse. These guys had the three basic ingredients for success: strong motivation with no fall back, charm personalities, and ability to do the work or find someone else to do the work.

### A Cautionary Tale
**The highest failure rate for prospective Indies is among "let go" executives from large companies.**

Here is the typical scenario:

Boss walks into your office and tells you "no more job," but either guilt or because he wants to tap out what you know, he says: "I would like to hire you to complete an assignment for me. I'll pay you a year's wages for the assignment and you have 6 months to complete it." (This is called an angel assignment).

You think: "Wow, this is great" and accept the assignment. You enjoy the work and the Indy lifestyle. You end the assignment and then your career as an Indy abruptly ends. Meanwhile you have left the corporate track and not pursued a career to which you might be better suited. An angel assignment is often the kiss of death for an aspiring Indy.

**If you are in this situation, immediately start looking for new business as soon as you leave your employer and follow the advice in this book on how to succeed as an Indy.**

---

### Work for a larger consulting firm

A lot of folks are recruited to work for medium and larger consulting firms. A few of these folks make a career of it, but most use it as a springboard to a promotion working for the Man. I have never known anyone who transitioned from working from a large consulting firm to becoming an independent consultant, but I guess it is possible. All of the people I have met at large consulting companies are herd people at heart. A large consulting company is just another name for the Man.

---

## Convert a "non-job" job into a consulting gig

The deadly combination of government overreach in regulating businesses and the decline in corporate morality in response to government policies that punish hiring employees has resulted in an explosion in the number and percent of "non-job jobs" such as contract employment or temp assignments and un-paid internships. Most companies do this, including the "do-good" companies.

Review any contract with an attorney before you sign any contractor agreement and follow the terms of the contract to the letter. If your contract allows you, search for and contract with other companies that may need your skill or expertise.

While you are "employed" in any type of "non-job," search for and contract with other companies that may need your skill or expertise.

The Man will discourage this behavior by probably having you sign some form of "exclusive use" type contract. I am not providing legal advice here but unless you reveal secrets you learn as a contractor or steal and then sell any company proprietary processes or procedures to another company, you will not have to worry about the Man coming after you. Why? Because slavery went out over a hundred and fifty years ago and courts/juries are loath to go after "runaway slaves." You are not worth the legal costs to go after and the contractor company probably would not want the negative publicity if they are caught going after you.

It is easy to become complacent and lazy, to not hustle up additional work while you are working as a non-employee employee for the Man, but you need to do it! The moral equation here is: the Man is screwing you by not giving you a real job, therefore it is ok that while you are working in the non-job job, the rule of thumb should be to do as little as possible and spend as little time as you can get away with in the non-job job and devote as much energy and time to your budding Indy career.

### Leaving the womb

At some time you have to cut the umbilical cord and leave the warm and comforting corporate/government world of steady paychecks. For several years before I decided to make the leap, I wanted to become an Indy but several things kept me in the corporate fold.
- Fear of the deep end
- Ignorance of "what do I do first"
- What's in a name?
- Where to work?
- What do I need?
- Money?

### Jumping into the deep end

When I was six years old my mother enrolled me in a swimming class. Learning to swim was the easy part. The hard part was jumping from the high board. From 10 feet up, the view to the bottom of the pool is 20 feet down, and I definitely did not want to jump. The instructor begged me and then called for my mother to come beg. I jumped! I think if my mother had said, "all right, you can climb down the ladder, and you can try it again when you are older," I never would have become an Indy let alone jumped from an airplane. **At some point you have to conquer your fears and just jump to leave the corporate world.**

### Who's on first?

Although I had attended business school and I had worked in business for several years, I did not actually know how to get started to run a business, so I hesitated to start my own business. The mechanics of starting an Indy business are remarkably easy.

In my area it was as easy as apple pie:
- Step One – registering the company name with the county registrar to obtain a "DBA" (doing business as)
- Step Two – Opening a checking account for the business
- Step Three – Starting a Quicken account for the business

- Step Four - When the first check came in, obtaining a business license from the city

In your area it may be a different process— so check with a business lawyer, bank and accountant. Also, depending upon your circumstances you should discuss various business forms such as Limited Liability Corporations with an attorney and/or a CPA.

The bottom line is: don't let concerns about the mechanics of starting a business deter you from making the jump.

### What's in a name?

Many folks get hung up on making the jump because they can't think of a really great name for their new business. Guess what: **company names don't mean much.** The only rule of thumb is: don't try to get too cute. Pick a name, any name! Here are some samples:
- Smith and Associates
- Smith Resources
- The Phoenix Consulting Group
- Smith and Company
- The Tech Group

### Where to work?

The great thing about consulting is that you can do it from anywhere. You can use a garage, a spare bedroom – a broom closet at a friend's business will all serve as your home office. I found that I needed separate space from my family to operate my business, but you may not.

### What do I need?

A telephone is all most Indies absolutely must own. Everything else you can hire – computer, printer, copier, etc. I managed my business from a European country for six months with nothing but a cell phone and a laptop. The point is, don't fear the need for "stuff" as a reason not to make the jump!

**Money**

I have been asked by prospective Indies "how much money should I have in savings before I make the jump?" The answer is that there are too many variables involved to give a number. As a very rough rule of thumb, I recommend about 1 year's salary plus make sure you cut out any discretionary spending prior to the jump.

## Chapter 4
# THE THREE TYPES OF INDIES

1. The "*consigliore*"

2. The technician

3. The case solver

**The Consigliore**

Think Tom in the movie *The Godfather*. A consigliore is a trusted advisor. The client will call the consigliore for advice or to attend meetings or deal with other problems. Often this is a role for a recently retired executive to help a former subordinate or protégé.

This is great work if you can get it! No papers to prepare, no presentations – just answer the phone and if necessary attend meetings. The consigliore is usually paid on a retainer basis for x number of days a month.

I have known this gig to last for a long time for one guy, but for the most part this is a short term opportunity because the client "grows up" and no longer needs the consigliore and the gig is not transferable to another company. Then you die. The key here is to continue to make the client believe that they are "still the kid" and need papa to succeed.

You can either use the consigliore as a great bridge between working for the Man and full retirement or as bridge to becoming a "case solver."

If you think you might want to become a consigliore make sure you are a great mentor/friend/lover of the folks in your current company – add up the favors other folks owe you. When you retire you will be surprised how few of the folks you were the mentor/friend/lover will hire you as a consigliore so make sure you wrap your arms around enough folks (and tightly) that one will hire you when you need him/her. Another trick is to keep a few pieces of the company puzzle in your pocket and dribble them out over time.

*The key to being a successful, long term consigliore is to always make the client look smarter than he/she is – without you, they just are not as smart- you are the difference between smart successful and not so smart failure.*

## Technician

A technician provides specific expertise the client does not possess in-house – think plug in, plug out – a new accounting wrinkle, a computer program, a transportation model, promotional materials, etc. The technician is paid a fixed price for the successful installation of the technical module. The problem of being a technician is you are one-and-done. You continually need to find new customers. You must keep your knowledge current and your knowledge can fairly quickly become obsolete.

Many technicians are "geeks" who lack most of the other Indy success variables. Most technicians only last a few years as an Indy. Although I knew one person who had a lengthy career as an ideation session moderator – he would roll in for two days of ideating and get paid $10,000. Nice work if you can get it. This gig lasted at least 20 years and may still be around even in the age of video-conferencing.

Here are a few keys to success as a technician.
1. Offer the clients "add-ons" to the original model – upgrades if you will.

2. Offer an "extended warranty" – like the creepy car companies.

3. Return to the client with "new and improved" models of your module.

4. **Try to figure out how to tie your module to "the bigger picture" at the client – to sell case solver work.**

5. Find out the client's need for other modules – you can act as a contractor for other technicians.

6. If you are a geek type technician – make sure you "polish yourself" per the advice offered in the success variables chapter in this book.

**The point is to not be lazy by just selling and installing your module!**

## Case Solver

Solving cases for clients is the best vehicle for being a true long term Indy. That's what I was. If you are old enough, you will remember *Mission Impossible* – Mr. Phelps was the case solver. He solved the client's problems with the right mixture of people and resources. A case solver lives on and on with a reputation for solving client problems rather than relying on a pal as a consigliore has to, or a module installer as a technician is perceived. Also, this is where the money is as the larger consulting firms have created a very rich pricing umbrella for this type of work. Where some large consulting firm would charge $500,000, I would charge $50,000 – the client was thrilled and I can guarantee you I was thrilled and my wife was thrilled. (See my discussion on you versus large consulting companies.)

Here are my hard earned lessons on being a successful case solver:
1. Start with a relatively narrow expertise – and expand it as you discover opportunities over time.

2. Sell all the way through the problem – background research, ideation, and implementation.

3. Achieve client buy-in to the project and its results.

4. Actually solve the problem as it is defined in the proposal.

5. Remember that you can virtually always find an expert to fill in the areas of expertise where you are lacking.

6. Look around a client company for people who need problems solved.

7. Be willing to solve the smallest of problems.

8. Look for problems the client does not even know exist and then solve them – also many clients vaguely know they have a problem but don't know how to articulate it or think it is unsolvable. Change their minds!

**How to solve a case**

Not many people can solve cases. I don't know why – it's not that tough.

Here is how you do it. Lay out all of the background material you have in hand, including what you acquired as part of your assignment. Then think of the three or four major conclusions that the data suggest and fill in the data to support each of the major conclusions – not rocket science. Here are the traps:

1. Not settling on what the key findings are – I call this the Hamlet mindset.

2. Letting your own prejudices overpower the data.

3. Fear of stepping on client prejudices – and sacred cows. I found that it is better to step on a few toes and risk enemies than not "telling it like it is."

4. Not getting all of the facts up front – and the right facts at that. I always believed the right facts were available if I looked hard enough and was willing to pay for them. I always tried to verify facts from more than one source.

5. Make sure you fit all of the facts neatly into your three or four conclusions. Once you have decided on your three or four major conclusions, look for additional data that supports those conclusions. Essentially, have an ironclad protection of your case solution, so that any "anti" person in your presentations cannot trip you up.

*Chapter 5*

# HOW TO "DRUM UP" BUSINESS

**Why Companies hire Indies**

To succeed as an Indy it is important to understand all of the motives companies have to hire an Indy and be able to satisfy them.

The obvious reason companies hire consultants is for specific expertise – both big consulting firms and Indies. But there are a variety of other reasons why companies hire consultants.

1. **Ego**. There is a big ego bounce for executives that hire "name" consulting firms. "Gee, "Biggie" is willing to help little ole me." Also, execs can take the Biggie's of the world to the Board. This is a huge selling point for the big consulting firms. As a side note, the most profitable clients for big consulting firms are the midsized companies where ego is a key selling variable. Most midsized companies do not know how to work with large consulting firms and the large consulting firms really know how to gouge these types of companies with exorbitant fees, add-ons and staffing by rookie MBAs. There is also substantial ego bounce (everyone likes their ass kissed now and then) to hiring an Indy- but not nearly as much as with a big consulting firm. This is a big distinction between the marketing and survival of an Indy and big consulting firms.

2. **Manpower** without the need to hire additional employees and the costs and hassles associated with them – essentially contract work

3. **Shoe leather** - At times it seemed to me that anyone could succeed as an Indy if they were willing to be a road warrior. This has become an increased reason to hire an Indy as women have moved into more senior positions at many companies. Many women past the age of 35 are loath to travel for more than a day or two at a time because of their children.

4. **Offloading unpleasant tasks** – affecting change and skewering sacred cows – support for a position to overcome objections or in political infighting.

5. **Shifting blame** if something could go wrong – not my fault, it was the lousy Indy.

6. **Shifting liability** – the hope is that the Indy will be sued and not the company.

7. **Cover** – so that customers and competitors will not learn "who is asking questions about them."

8. **Budget** – most mid-level and a bit higher managers have discretionary funds budgets – money they can spend on stuff without any questions. Execs like this independence and will defend it. Much of that money can go to Indies because if the exec does not spend the discretionary funds they are taken away.

9. **A good friend** – a good Indy will exploit a client's need for a confidant, someone who will be fascinated by his life and play golf with him.

10. **Providing support** for the client's position in meetings with subordinates and superiors. The Indy's role is the "amen sayer" to whatever the client says.

**Why companies ditch Indies – and how to beat it.**
1. You screw-up – you deserve to be ditched.

2. You forget or ignore all the success keys to being an Indy – not my fault!

3. The bosses say "we need to cut consulting fees" – I found a way to beat this: have your client define you as "research" rather than consulting. For some reason bosses are loath to cut research but eager to cut consulting.

4. A big consulting firm comes in and eats up all of the available funds for consultants.

5. The client contact leaves his/her position, for example: retirement, transfer, promotion, fired, quits. This can be a killer. Here are some ways to combat this:
   a. Always romance and create goodwill with potential replacement folks at the client.
   b. Always try to keep some type of assignment going so that if a new person comes in you will have the opportunity to create a working relationship with him/her.
   c. Don't become too associated as the client contact's "man" – you need to be thought of, as much as possible, as the company's man.
   d. Communicate with the replacement your historic contribution to the now departed guy – and your crucial contribution to the departing guys' success. Force an appointment!

**How to attract customers**
1. Arrange to speak at trade conferences. The topic should essentially be a teaser of your expertise – attendees will need to hire you to "get the real answers." Obtain a list of attendees and follow up with them.

2. Publish articles in trade publications – again the topic should be a teaser.

3. Tap out all contacts in your field – cold call. This is the tough one for most people: swallowing your pride and reaching for the telephone – If you have nothing else to do.

4. Send out cold letters/proposals on ideas that a potential client could use. Example: "Hi Joe, I was thinking today about your need to rethink your truck routing – perhaps the Zither program might work for you. I have tried it at Xenix Industries and they are raving about it – give me a call and let's chat."

## How to expand business at current clients

I always considered the first assignment at a client to be a hunting license for more business throughout the client company. Here are a few tricks:

1. If I was doing business with one product manager I would go around to the office of every other product manager and if the person was in the office I would chat (read: tell them about how great the assignment was going and imply that "my" product manager was "getting a leg up" on other product managers using my work) about my current assignment and ask for business from that person. If the office was empty I would pick up a business card and leave mine. Follow up with a letter and send a brochure – or e-mail and mention your website.

2. Ask your client contact if other people at his/her level need your services – then call on the person recommended.

3. Encourage the client to include as many people as possible at your presentation. Introduce yourself to all attendees – you never know if any of the attendees will give you business. Write thank you notes to all attendees for attending your presentation, remarking on how valuable their input was.

4. Most clients will pigeonhole you as an expert in a very narrow way – try to expand that pigeonhole. Listen carefully for the client to tell you of a need for consulting in an area just outside your pigeonhole – and tell them you can do it.

5. Add extras to your existing service. For example if I did an industry study, I would then tell the client I could translate that to a strategy plan, and then I would tell them I could help them execute the plan, and then I told them I could conduct the sales training program.

6. Try to get bigger paying assignments by moving up the chain of command – if you start with a product manager who is paying you $10,000, try to get an assignment from a group product manager for $30,000 or the VP Marketing for $100,000. I always liked to start fairly low in an organization where it was possible to gain a toehold at the client and then move up in the organization.

**Forcing new business/selling**
1. Cold calling

Cold calling is the process of telephone calling, e-mailing and/or other electronic communications or snail mail. This is what telephone solicitors do – think stock brokers. Cold calling works for an Indy if he/she has any excuse (real or imagined) to contact a prospective client. Here are some examples of cold call excuses:

"When I presented at the conference you filled out a form asking for more information"

"Joe Schmoo, the president of your company, suggested I contact you regarding your expansion plans"

"I read the article you wrote in Modern Technology and I have a couple of questions"

"I am an expert in the spaghetti industry and recently completed work for Ace Sauce Company – I think your pepperoni company could use what I know."

Here are some pointers:

- Be creative and stretch the truth! Perhaps you sat next to Joe Schmoo on a flight and he said to talk to one of his people – as a brush off – doesn't matter, Joe told you to contact people in his company!
- Be persistent! – keep contacting until you get a response.
- Accept rejection- multiple times – all you need is one or two hits to survive – think the prospect of 100 calls for every hit.
- In the old days, the key to success in cold calling was to romance a secretary, gatekeeper – probably not very effective anymore but some places it still works, particularly when cold calling senior executives who still have secretaries.
- Broadcast via electronic mail or snail mail a brochure or virtual brochure to prospective clients. Mailing lists could include such sources as attendees at conferences, or trade shows, people mentioned in trade publications, etc.
- At trade shows walk around to the booths of companies you might want to contract some work and ask for the level person who might be able to contract with you – then buttonhole them. Usually the time to do this is the first day of the show when more senior people attend and they are still fresh and eager.
- Anything but "no" is a yes! So, "maybe", "perhaps", "someday" or "I'll think about it" are door openers – push the door open all the way!

Cold calling is not very productive, but if you have nothing else to do, you need to cold call – it could keep you alive as an Indy. Think of yourself as Yogi Bear – cold callings are the nuts and berries between the picnic baskets and dumpsters. For encouragement, I once worked with a guy who was a master cold caller and stayed in business as an Indy a long time despite his other numerous shortcomings as an Indy.

Even when you become rich and famous you need to cold call – it will keep you sharp and is the best medicine against "I'm great" hubris!

2. Cold proposals

You have a brilliant idea you think other people will want to pay for – send out "cold proposals." Once you send the proposal, follow up with calls. I believe in sending cold proposals to fairly high level executives such as a VP Manufacturing or even to a president. If the addressee does not trash the proposal, he/she will send it to a subordinate. When you call the big magoo, the secretary will say that big magoo sent your proposal to Joe Glutz. You than call Joe Glutz stating that Mr. Magoo "asked me to call you to follow up on the proposal" you sent.

Cold proposals are productive- particularly if you are an idea oriented Indy.

3. Forced meetings

Forced meetings can work, particularly if you live near your prospective client base – "I am in your lobby (pick the fabricated reason why you are in the lobby) and if you have a few moments I would like to introduce myself, etc.

Also, many times, a combination of all of the three forms of cold calling methods are needed to succeed. One time I sent a cold proposal to a prospective client and then left a voice mail with him that I would call on him at 9:00 am the following Tuesday when I was visiting St. Louis on other client business. I told the receptionist I had an appointment with the prospective client and walked in his office at 9:00 am. He said: "who are you and what are you doing in my office?" I told him about the proposal – which, of course he had trashed – and then proceeded to pitch him on what a great opportunity if was for him. He answered: "Great, let's do it." I almost fainted – it was one the biggest pieces of business I ever contracted up to that date, and it opened a new line of business for me.

## Leverage your time

Leveraging your time means that you essentially earn more money for the same amount of time you devote to your work. Here are a few ways to do it:

**Hire sub-contractors** - A great source for me were just retired executives in the industry I was conducting my work. Actually, the best time to hire them is about a year after they have retired and are bored to death – golf everyday is not as great as they thought when they were working. They will work for a small fee and they probably know everyone in the industry. One of the keys in hiring sub-contractors is not to teach them to be competitive with you – very carefully firewall the entire project from a sub-contractor.

**Sell multi-client reports/studies**. With the multi-client study, you tell the clients that the report will be sold to a number of clients to reduce the cost to any one client. Let's say you cost out a project at $50,000. You think you could sell the project at $20,000 to five clients. You will more than break even at three clients and hit pay-dirt with the four or more. Also, multi-client studies open the door for the Indy at a variety of clients for future work. You can "personalize" the study for a client for an additional fee. Needless to say – I loved multi-client work!

**Recycle existing work**

I've seen this done a lot particularly by bigger consulting firms. They take a study for one client and repackage it for another. The bigger firms use this trick primarily because a client cannot afford the real going rate for biggy firms. I have never liked this as I think it is dishonest and it usually shows as shoddy work as each client is slightly different. If you get found out recycling existing work your Indy career is toast.

## Chapter 6
# WHAT ARE THE INDY TRAPS

1. **Falling in love with your own ideas.** You are in the idea selling business not the "invest in ideas" business.

2. **Being happy with just one client.**
   - You will get sloppy over time and start to act like an employee
   - Your angel will leave the company
   - The love affair ends – and you have forgotten how to hustle business

3. **Limiting yourself to too narrow a niche of expertise.** Times change and technologies change so that you want to be an expert on Windows not just Windows8. On the other hand don't wander too far away from your niche – be an expert on Windows, not all computer programs. You need to put serious thinking time against this issue by noting changes in demand for your specific expertise and forecast where technology and fashion in your industry is going. I became an expert in about 4 different fields over the life of my consulting career.

4. **Forgetting what side of the desk you are sitting on.** Remember that that it is the client's ego that needs stroking and not yours. I like the expression in the movie Cool Hand Luke – "pickin' it up boss." On your side of the desk you have to kiss butt.

## Kissing Butt – a primer

To succeed as an Indy, you need to kiss butt – **meaning you absolutely need to check your ego at the door.** Here are a number of ways you will need to kiss butt – but (excuse the pun) I am sure there are many more.

- The client is always right.
- The client is also more: smart, funny, manly (goes for men and women), athletic, attractive, likeable, moral, interesting, and powerful, than you are.
- The client can be late – you never can be.
- The client can say jump and your answer is always "how high."
- The client picks the restaurant and the table and sets the example of what to eat and you pay the bill.
- The client makes a mistake, then it is your fault.
- You can be the butt of the client's jokes, but not vice versa.
- The client's ethnicity, gender, school and school athletics, sexual orientation are superior to yours.
- The client's favorite team is superior to yours.
- The client tells a joke and you laugh.
- The client's family is interesting and yours isn't.
- The client can change meeting dates, times, and anything else to accommodate him/her – you guessed it, you can't.
- You always return phone calls, etc. immediately. The client may or may not do the same – probably not unless he/she wants something.
- You rise from your chair when the client enters the room and greet him/her and behave as though his/her arrival is the highlight of your day – the client will not reciprocate!
- When the client calls you sound like it is the highlight of your day to hear his/her voice.
- The amount of butt kissing you need to do is a function of how in demand your services/advice is – if you possess the secrets to eternal youth, no butt kissing is required.

Your ego is only truly stroked by five things – in order:

- ✓ When the client's check clears the bank – savor the moment.

- ✓ When the client hires you for the next job – see #1.
- ✓ Any words of praise or thanks from the clients for the work you have done – only value when it translates to #2, so don't let it get to your head. Compliments are always answered with a smile and a thank you.
- ✓ The quality of your life.
- ✓ Whenever I had to KB with a client, I realized that as soon as I left him/her, I didn't have to kiss anybody's butt, but the client had to KB his boss every day!

This was the hardest part of being an Indy for me and frankly no matter how hard I tried I was only mediocre at it. The larger my net worth became, the harder it became for me to pucker up – "I am worth $XX million, why do have to kiss some doofus's butt! The answer was always, because if you don't you will no longer be an Indy. As I mentioned in the introduction to the book, this is one of the main reasons I retired from being an Indy.

It is also one of the reasons so few people last as Indies. On the one hand you need to have a pretty strong ego to tell other people what to do and to stand in front of an audience and present a report when the audience might be throwing spears at you and at the same time bury your ego with the client.

The BK is also one of the reasons why former senior executives at companies invariably fail as Indies –not because they lack knowledge, but because they cannot flip from having their butts kissed to becoming a butt kisser.

5. **Spending as if you "have it made."** Always have a financial cushion and spend well below what you make. You may think you have it made after a good year or two, but a little bad luck and you could throw craps and go a long time without an assignment. I once went 6 months between assignments and without a cushion. I would have been dead meat. Once, after two great years, I thought I had it made. My wife and I headed to the Jaguar dealer in town and took a test drive. Fortunately my wife did not like the head room in the car and we didn't purchase it. But the very fact that we test-drove the Jag resulted in a very poor year

after that. Maybe there was cause and effect, I don't know, but from that day forward, I drove a Toyota.

6. **Portraying a lifestyle greater than your clients.** I think portraying a lifestyle slightly lower than your client's is the best attitude. If he/she belongs to a fancy golf club, yours is a little less fancy. If he drives a 700 series BMW, you drive a 500 series, etc. In a way it makes you appear as if the client is what you aspire to. I happen to live in a resort town destination. This presented a problem for clients who might be located in Cincinnati, Ohio. Early in my career I was stupid enough to tell a client how glorious the weather was when they asked about it during telephone calls. I finally figured out the best answer was "hot as blazes" or has "rained for ten straight days and oops, that earthquake sure rattled me."

7. **Getting into the game of "I am smarter than you."** This is a tricky one and one I was not very good at it. The problem is that your client is paying you for your smarts – smarts he or she may not possess, but the client does not want to feel intellectually inferior. The obvious solution is to appear not as smart as the client in everything except the area where you are the expert. I have found that it is helpful to compliment the client in areas where they think they are superior to you. For example, charisma, people skills, number crunching, etc

8. **Appearing to be out of date or "not with it."** Keep an ear open for the latest business buzz words particularly in your field of expertise. Also keep abreast of current fashion trends and current events, particularly sports. Try to dress like the clients do – perhaps a little more formally.

9. **Adding overhead that is absolutely not needed.** You should be very disciplined about adding any expense – remember that one of the key advantages of being an Indy is low overhead. Any over head item reduces your take-home. On the other hand, stay

"electronically hip." That is, use the latest presentation equipment or software and be able to interface with client electronics – but don't waste money on gee-gaws and computer/electronic stuff you don't need. Think very seriously about hiring anyone – if you need to use other people's talent, hire it on a contracting basis where every possible.

10. **Thinking you are a genius because other people are paying you for your brains or what you know.** This is a huge trap – the smartest guys I know have the worst judgment and have done the dumbest things – this is what the ancient Greeks called hubris. Rather than thinking I am the smartest, I hire the smartest CPAs, attorneys, electricians, and plumbers. The key is to listen carefully to experts and continue to learn from others.

11. **Losing focus on your objective:** keeping as much money for you and your family as you can! Losing focus on that includes thinking you are doing societal good, empathizing with client's problems, feeding your ego. Remember: to live the life of an Indy is to be the quintessential Machiavellian! Here is an example. I was working with a long term client and figured out I had tapped him out for as much work at that company as I could. So I convinced him he could probably make more money at another firm and to start interviewing. He got a new job and used me for the exact same work he contracted at his old job. This extended my revenue with this guy for another five years. I always encouraged people to change companies either if they could not spend money or if I had tapped them out.

12. **Forgetting your role model – a jackal – when you start thinking like a wildebeest or a lion.** Wildebeest are the prey and they have prey mind set – if you think you are a lion you will go hungry! You may get lucky and kill a wildebeest or come upon a wildebeest carcass, but over time you will stay alive by hunting rabbits, crickets and nuts and berries.

13. **Attaching yourself to the client's use of your project.** Only take pride in the work you do – try to do your best possible work, but then let go of it. There is a high probability that a client will screw up whatever you provide them or not take your advice at all. The best piece of work I ever put together provided a clear road map for a client to win in a new market but a few months later a big consulting firm convinced the client to not enter the market. The point is that you will go nuts and lose interest in being an Indy if you attach your ego to the client's use of your product.

14. **Confusing "managing your business" with consulting.** Managing your business includes such tasks as fixing your computer, filling out expense reports, making travel plans, preparing tax returns. Think of it this way: the time you spend managing your business is non billable. It does not add new clients or complete work – essentially it is a waste of productive time. I tried to never do any business management chores during regular business hours – do them at night rather than watch television or on weekends. Only do them during business hours if you truly have nothing else to do.

15. **Confusing real knowledge and expertise with knowledge and expertise with extraneous stuff such as fiddling with electronic gadgets and technology.**

16. **Developing hubris:** overrating your talents and skills – most long term Indies that suffer from hubris flame out in their business and their personal lives.

17. **Hiring employees!** The rule of thumb is: don't. Obviously, in some situations or types of consulting you may need to hire employees and employees can leverage your time, but remember:

- Never hire employees as an ego trip – for example a receptionist/assistant. I know of two Indies who hired employees to massage their egos – one learned his lesson and fired the employee and the other went down in flames while still maintaining "staff."
- Employees are a fixed cost while your income will be variable – trust me, at some point in time you will roll craps and not have any income for a long period of time while payroll keeps on ticking. Make sure you have a really steady stream of income before you hire an employee.
- Think of all the government work rules and potential costs associated with firing, sexual harassment, etc.
- Employees need time and energy to manage – skills you may not possess.
- Always try to contract work rather than hire a person!

18. **All the Internet wastes of time, including games, texting your pals, fantasy football, Facebook, etc. are now toast!** Get rid of them unless they directly relate to your business or your other moral objective, i.e., family time. Also, iPod and other listening devices: gone. You should be thinking about building your business and solving your client's cases. Perhaps I am overstating this point, but it is very important to substitute waste-of-time activity with productive activity.

19. **Last, but certainly not least, is letting the "socially negative" requirements of your Indy persona intrude on your relationships with friends, neighbors and relatives – they are not the prey! You will always have to work on this.**

## Chapter 7
## STAYING ALIVE!

Obviously, the key to succeeding as an Indy for a long period of time is to keep the gig going through "thick or thin." The following is a list of all of the tricks I learned to "stay alive".

1. Even if you think you have nothing to do, spend at least 4 hours a day in your office – boredom/anxiety (oh shit, I am sitting here with nothing to do, "I am screwed") will eventually force you to do the things that are the hardest for you such as cold calling or cold letters, taking care of business details, or even thinking of new ideas.

2. Think/worry about your business 24 hours a day! We are talking obsessive compulsive here - I always worried about solving a case or how to complete a report. I usually "wrote" my next day's work during my sleep – never experienced writer's block. Speaking of writer's block, if you have it at all, just write something - even if it is gibberish. Just the process of writing will get you going. Great vacations, time consuming hobbies (golf, sailing) are the releases for wildebeests – your satisfactions come from the check arriving in the mail and the Zen from the quality of the work you produce. I didn't take a vacation for 17 years – I know of one Indy that never took a vacation and had zero hobbies. He believed that even serving on jury duty was contrary to the code of a successful Indy. Always worry about money and your future success – if you don't, both will disappear.

3. Here is a tip I learned early on: every Friday afternoon, get out a yellow pad of paper and think about and write down all of the things you think you should accomplish the next week. On Monday morning you will have your marching orders for the week and you will be prepared to hit the ground running. Check off each item on your sheet of paper as you accomplish each item. This was a key success variable for me.

4. Stay healthy – you're the only machine in your factory – you go down, the business goes down.
    - Work out an hour a day – walking/ pumping iron. I lived on the west coast and most of my clients were on the east coast, so any time after 2:30 I could work out. Working out not only keeps you fit, it also helps to relieve stress and allows you to think about what you will be doing the next day. Watch the food intake – it is very easy for an Indy to put on weight because of the close proximity of a kitchen/refrigerator.
    - Give yourself breaks – rewards – while you are working.

5. Always under promise and over deliver.

6. Always be on time – date of delivery, meetings, etc.

7. Avoid burnout – burnout as an Indy is a huge occupational hazard – the demands to deliver, travel, playing the ego game, the 24/7 attention to winning. This was a key success variable for me.

Here are a few tips:
- Think of your job as a game – you win every time a check arrives in the mail.
- Engage in low time requirement hobbies – I worked in the garden, painted my house and played tennis.
- Revel in the benefits of being an Indy and think about what clients are doing – sitting in meetings!

- Talk out your frustrations with a friend, spouse or shrink.

8. Minimize the burdens of travel:

If you haven't traveled extensively for business, you might think that life on the road is fun and romantic. After about a year as an Indy, if you are normal, you will discover it's an incredible pain in the ass. Forget the movie *Up in the Air* – trust me, even if you are George Clooney – there is virtually no chance for a sex life while you are on the road! As an aside: I actually have known Indies who thrive on travel –essentially to get away from family to smoke, drink and frequent strip clubs.

I am sure there are a number of books devoted to instructing readers how play the road warrior game. I suggest you read one. Here are just a few road warrior pointers that might not be in one of those books.

**Try to locate your Indy business near your clients or live near a hub airport, preferably in the eastern Midwest. I paid a heavy price for living in a city far away from the majority of my clients.**

- Join airline clubs.
- Upgrade when/where possible.
- Use limos/cabs rather than drive.
- Start your trip from a hub – not a spoke. I live in a spoke location but would take a shuttle van/bus to a hub location because of the larger number of available flights and to reduce the possibility of mechanical difficulties or weather delays on one more leg of air travel.
- If you have jet lag, don't perform any serious work the day you return home – particularly writing.
- Avoid any menu item that includes the words marinated and hollandaise sauce.

9. Always say yes to clients' requests. I remember one time a client needed some information and she only had $250 to pay me. I said I would be delighted to help – $250 paid for a week's worth of groceries (at the time) and I was a hero to the client when the client was in a jam. This client rewarded me with business for many years.

10. **"Keep your chin up." You will have a number of highs and lows during your Indy career.** It is difficult to not beat yourself up for mistakes. I still do it even though I have been retired for a while. It is easy to get discouraged when you haven't seen a check for a few months or have lost a key client. Consulting is very much like baseball – you will have great streaks and prolonged slumps. **The key to success (life) is to muddle through.**

11. Minimize the impact of competition. Here's how:

---

### The Big Guys

You can't beat the Big Guy so as a rule of thumb, don't try. While the Big Guy is at your client, stay in touch with the client but stay out of the way. But think of the Big Guys as lions who kill wildebeests – they usually leave behind plenty of food for the nimble jackal – you the Indy.

Here are the nice pieces of meat left behind by the lions:
- A humbler client – who has been had by the glitzy name of the big consulting firm – paid big bucks for a bunch of rookie MBAs who mucked around in their company.
- A client who will appreciate your value more – after they have been gouged by the Big Guys, you can charge them more.
- Most large consulting firms are formulaic – I used to call it the gloppidy-glop machine. Big firms need formulas both as a point of differentiation from other big firms and to maintain quality and consistency throughout their large organizations. The formula is the "secret sauce" that they tell clients is the wizardry they bring to the table. The problem is that "the formula" is usually too rigid to work for individual cases and Big Guys dump all the data (good, bad and irrelevant) into the machine. The end result in many cases is shoddy work that will make your past work look better and encourage the client to employ you forever.

- Most large consulting firms leave behind unfinished work and confused and frustrated client workers – you, the Indy can clean up and tie up all of the loose ends and pick the bones clean!

Here's how to handle the Big Guys

I found it is never a good idea to bad mouth a Big Guy the client's senior management has brought in. Here are relationship phases with the client and the Big Guys and how you deal with them.

---

Romance Phase

When clients first hire a Big Guy it is true love – particularly with senior management, the level where the Big Guys sell. So this is the time to stay away from the client and only maintain client contact on a "friend" basis.

---

Disillusionment Phase

During this phase, continue to stay away – far away. Again chat with your client on a friend basis – appear surprised at the problems they are having with the Big Guy. Avoid the temptation to offer suggestions or bad mouth the Big Guy!

---

"Woe is me" Phase

In this phase, the client will usually feel used and abused. This is the phase to reengage with the client – offering help to solve problems or straighten out the mess the Big Guy has created. Since the Big Guy has probably eaten up the client's budget for consulting, ease in with lower cost projects – or suggest the client pay you from different accounts such as "research" accounts

## Other service companies

Other service companies include advertising agencies, accounting firms, promotional agencies, and a host of others. These guys you can bad mouth (subtly), essentially telling the client the service company lacks your specific expertise and/or intelligence and about the service company's "greed motivation" to stretch their expertise at the client' expense. Service companies are very scared of losing their clients so I preyed on this fact by intimating that if they messed with my business at the client I would reciprocate in spades.

## New little guys

These are your bitter enemies – where possible, squash them like a bug! Truly, it is the law of the jungle: every dollar they earn in your field will come almost exclusively from your pocket. Here are a few tips on how to handle little guys

- **Never, ever encourage someone to become an Indy in your field** – for instance, client people who are looking for a change. If they really want to become a consultant, encourage them to work for a Big Guy to "learn how to become a consultant" and the steady paycheck.
- Never flash or talk about how much money you are making.
- Emphasize how difficult it is to be an Indy – read off the negatives of being an Indy described earlier.
- Intimate/communicate that you have your niche entirely in your pocket.
- Patent/copyright anything that is proprietarily yours - aggressively go after anyone pirating your materials.
- The best defense is to maintain broad and deep relationships with your clients and other companies that are in your niche.
- **Avoid the temptation to give advice to a new Indy.** I have known Indies who have let their ego take control and give

struggling new Indies advice and then rue the day! Your advice should always be for the new Indy to get out!

---

## **Other Indies**

Indies are like wolf packs – they tend to stay out of another pack's territory – but not always. Many times a client will hire two Indies to keep the resident Indy "honest" or another executive at the client company will bring in an Indy. Here are some tips to handle other Indies:
- Always be nice and respectful of them when you see them at the client.
- Always ask to see their work so you can "review it" – then subtly destroy or denigrate it.
- Limit the scope and range of the other Indy – contain the damage.
- Subtly indicate to the client that you may drop the client because of the lack of billings – another company/competitor has been pressuring you to work for that company. Essentially this is the "he goes or I go" strategy.
- If you are new at a client who already has an Indy, try to stay under the radar scope and avoid the resident Indy. Become "indispensable" with the client before you try to oust the resident Indy.

12. Manage the "imposition."

The imposition is when your client is (for example) the VP Marketing and he "imposes" you on his staff. During most of my career my clients were at the operational level – brand managers, sales managers and the like. But late in my career I was contracting with VPs and higher.

**The general reaction to an imposition by staff is negative** – "why do we need the consultant?" The implication is that the boss does not have confidence in his/her staff to solve a problem.

What works with the staff folks is the application of the old "carrot and the stick." At its extreme, the carrot is "I will make you look like a hero, get you promoted and you will live happily ever after. The extreme stick is "I'll get your sorry ass fired and you will die in dire poverty." The amount of carrot and stick you use is dependent on the reaction of the individual staff members to you.

---

Passive Accepters

The passive acceptors will go along and get along. Most folks are passive acceptors. They just need a little carrot and just the hint of possible stick.

---

Active rejecters

Most of these folks are tied in with Other Service companies, such as the advertising agency with the Ad Manager, or the marketing research agency with the Market Research Manager. The "other service companies have their noses buried so far up their clients butts they touch the lower intestine – so the staff person upon whom you are imposed is going to fight you all the way. I found that only the stick of using the boss to impose "you will cooperate" works with active rejecters.

I recommend that before you meet with the boss's staff you:

1. Try to get a "lay of the land" from your client about his/her people and the political environment you are entering.
2. Read body language and reactions from staff members to determine where the staff member is an accepter or a rejecter
3. Determine the exact amount of carrot and stick to apply to each staff member.
4. Understand the management style of the boss, your client.

---

Participatory

Everyone chats and a "consensus is reached" – go heavy on the carrots.

Fake Participatory
>   Everyone chats and then the boss says: "This is what we will do" – (watch for a fake out here) – blend of carrot and stick as the troops usually think they have real power.

Autocrat
>   The boss asks for specific opinions from staff and then tells everyone what to do and when to do it – use the big stick.

13. The three legged stool

Fairly early on I learned the lesson that to stay in business I needed to maintain a stable of three clients. Any more than three and it became unmanageable and I would lack the time to continue to market my business. I would be spending all my time on client work and no time in trying to get new clients – then when the work ran out on the current clients, I would theoretically be out of business.

Anything less than three clients and any sort of bad luck or timing and I would again be out of business. The way to look at it is this:
- More than three clients: will work if you can sub out the work – entirely
- Three clients: the sweet zone – but always fear losing any client
- Two clients: worry and hustle
- One client: an invitation to disaster – hustle your butt off

A gray area here is how do you treat different departments at one client? Treat them all as one client – because if one big magoo doesn't want you around, you are toast in the company – period.

Another gray area is working as a subcontractor – initially do not count this as a client – but once you have a multi assignment relationship, treat "the contractor" as a client. Here is a big warning: When I was subbing, the contractor had multiple clients, but the contractor became my only client – when my relationship with the contractor ended, he had the clients and I was out of luck.

14. Subcontracting

Subcontracting is an important component of staying in business as an Indy - that has many risks and rewards – you can sub out your services or hire subcontractors.

**You, the subcontractor**
**The rewards**
- It's money.
- You don't have to spend any time or effort to attract a client – the contractor does that.
- The contractor manages the client and usually makes the presentation.
- The contractor may have skills you don't possess and you need them – for example the contractor may be a super salesman and you aren't.
- You can learn a ton from subcontracting with others. I learned almost everything about consulting working with other firms- what they did right and what they did wrong.
- You will gain access to new clients when the contractor brings you into presentations or lets you present or you work with client people – by the way, make sure you come along on contractor presentations.
- Often consultants at bigger consulting firms cross over to work for client companies and will engage you to perform consulting services for them.

**The pitfalls**
- You have to wait for the pay – the client pays the contractor and then the contractor pays you.
- The contractor is not a big company and he/she may cheat you. It happened to me in a big way once – I was supposed to be paid ½ of billings, but the contactor lied about the sizes of contracts.
- The contractor usually makes much more money on a job even though the sub might do most of the work.
- The contractor may steal/use your techniques, processes or style and then discard you once they have picked you dry.

- You will need to satisfy both the client and the contractor- and often that can be a conflict. You may face a moral dilemma when you discover that the consultant is flat out wrong and the result will be a substantial loss for the client. It happened to me at least twice in my career.
- The contractor owns the client not you – so it is difficult to have strong relationships at a client.
- You will need to kiss the contractor's butt as if they are a client.
- Often contractors do not get their feet wet in the actual work and will not support you in front of the client or they may even appear disinterested. It is important to involve the contractor in the work even if it is just to "proofread" your work.
- You get lazy and fail to hustle your own business.
- You can become the scapegoat for the contractor for anything that the client doesn't like – "gee, it was my supplier's fault - I will never use him again."

Here's the deal: Because I lacked super interpersonal skills and where I lived was far from customer bases, I spent much of my career as a subcontractor. It was a huge price. Trust me, it is much, much better and more rewarding to have your own clients.

Here are some tricks to minimize the negatives of working as a sub:

- Try to minimize subbing to less than 50% of your billings.
- Try not to share any of your proprietary knowledge with the contractor.
- Absolutely do not let the contractor monopolize your time.
- Hire a lawyer to develop a written contract – your word may be your bond, but don't expect if of the contractor.
- Remember that the contractor needs you or he would not be hiring you - you are overhead – so don't be a wuss on fees.
- When the contractor first hires you it will be true love, but over time the bloom will leave the rose and they will think they don't need you – particularly if they suck you dry of your expertise.
- Try to learn what the contractor is being paid by the client so you can learn how much to charge the contractor.

- Ingratiate yourself with contractor client (but don't backstab the contractor).

**Hiring subcontractors**

I used a lot of subcontractors over the years – with very positive results.

Here is what I learned
- There is plenty of expertise out there – and it is not hard to find. The best sources are the recently retired and the recently fired. They have the expertise, knowledge of their industry and have always dreamed of being a consultant.
- Some subs I never had to pay money – just had to stoke their egos by telling them how smart or knowledgeable they were.
- Subs almost always charge way less than their value. Some subs would work for peanuts just for the frequent flyer/stayer points associated with consulting travel. For many retirees with a pretty good pension, a few thousand bucks and a few thousand points were plusses in their lives. Also, it was great for the ego to say to their friends they were now consultants rather than retirees/unemployed.
- Try to never bring them to meet clients unless you absolutely need them there.
- Try not to tell the sub who the client is.
- **Pay fast and per the contract.**
- Subs provide great "cut-outs." Let's say that the client needs information about a competitor. The client uses you to get the data and puts in writing that you must be moral and legal, but winks and really does not (want to) know how you got the data. You can then do the same thing with a sub – when/if the shit hits the fan, the sub is the guy holding the bag.
- **Treat any sub with respect and lavish with praise - Don't be chicken shit with a sub.**

15. Client contact - Here are some general rules:
- Maintain continual contact with a client. Contact around once every two weeks – more than that you seem like a pest, and less

- than that you start to lose contact. Find an excuse, any excuse, for the contact.
- I may be old fashioned, but I believe in telephone or face to face contact rather than electronic contact. Why? Here are just a few of the reasons – real time dialogue, emotional context, tone of voice, spontaneity.
- My rule of thumb is that electronic contact should only be as an augmentation to telephone or face to face contact and specifically as a cover for sending electronic files and documenting verbal agreements or facts.
- Also, wear your big boy pants/skirts and handle an unhappy or angry client via telephone or face to face – let them vent and you express your heartfelt "I'm sorry!" rather than copout with electronic communications. The client will almost always go over the top with unhappy or angry comments and will "feel guilty" when you express your abject humility and "sorry-ness" and it will usually improve your relationship with the client.
- Face to face contact is by far the best contact – in office, on the golf course, restaurants, bars, motels, shared flights, etc.
- **When you contact the client by telephone make sure it is on Tuesday through Thursday – never, never on Monday.** Friday is a waste of time – Tuesday morning is the best. Try to be the first call of the day for the client – If I knew the client usually arrived at work at 8:30am, I would start calling at 8:20 – and keep calling until the client answered – always the first call. Never call after lunch.
- The client should always be able to reach you (this means always! – during vacations, holidays, family events) and if you miss a call or other communication, return the communication as soon as possible. With call waiting, always take a client call over a personal call.
- Send e-mails in the evening so that your e-mail is the first one the client sees in the morning before they are angry about all the e-mails and junk mail they have to deal with.
- Use the U.S. Mail or express mail – on quality stationary or card stock for formal documents and personal notes such as

condolence notes, congratulations, and thank-you notes. Because snail mail is now rare, it has greater impact than other forms of communication.
- Always have the character to take a client call – even if you know they are not happy with you or are, in fact, angry with you.

16. Treat a client as if he/she is a great friend. I recommend creating a contact file for each client that includes everything I ever learned about a client including children's names ages and interests. If possible, always weave this information into any communication with clients.

17. I learned that it is a good idea to "give back to clients" in the form of small year-end holiday gifts. I also provided clients and their friends and family tennis lessons. Another Indy offered golfing "stop-overs" at his golf club for clients. Another Indy just happened to have a couple of extra tickets for major sporting events.

# Chapter 8
# HOW TO PREPARE WINNING PROPOSALS

The proposal is first and foremost a selling document to convince the prospective client of the following:
1. To contract an outsider for consulting work
2. That you are the best person to do the work
3. The process you want to use is correct to solve the client's problem
4. To pay you fairly for the work you will do
5. To agree on a timeline for the work you will perform

Proposals are what I did best and kept me alive. I only lost one or two jobs over 35 years to competing proposals. So pay attention boys and girls!

Here are so general tips:
- **The sine qua non of writing winning proposals is to obtain exact clarity from the client what they want, when they want it and how much money they have to spend to get what they want.** This is not as easy as it sounds as many times I found that

clients were not entirely sure what they wanted and were vague when I asked them exactly what they wanted. You need to force clarity!

Here is a typical interview format:

> You: "Tell me what you need."
>
> Client: "I need xyz"
>
> You: "when would you like it?"
>
> Client: "In three months"
>
> You: "From what you have told me, I think the cost will be about $XX – does this fit your budget for the assignment?"
>
> Client: "Yes"
>
> You: Let me summarize what you have told me you want. You want xyz completed in three months and the prospective price I mentioned fits your budget. "Is this correct?"
>
> Client: "Yes"

- The first thing to remember is that a proposal, when it is accepted is a contract, so it must have the elements of a contract – including deliverables, timing and price.
- If possible, never use conditional words in a proposal! For example, always use "will" rather than "could" or "might."
- Avoid long sentences at all costs, and break paragraphs so they are never than an inch deep when printed in 14 point.
- Although you might possess a mastery of the English language and can dazzle people with your vocabulary, stick to commonly used words usually with no more than two syllables.
- Use footers with a title of the assignment, date, page number and your company name – this helps the client and gives a prospective bidding competitor pause before they rip off your proposal.
- Absolutely make sure there are no spelling, grammar or layout errors in a proposal.
- **Always get money up front** – generally in the form of a "project inception fee" – will discuss later.
- Proposals can be written or oral – but they should both have the following components:

## The "Background Statement"

**The background statement is the most important part of an entire project!** When writing a proposal, I would spend about 70% of my time writing the background statement and 30% on the rest of the proposal.

The background statement includes four elements.

1. Who the client is – who wants the work

2. What the client wants - exactly

3. Why they want it.

4. A reason to buy now

The reason the lead sentence is the most important sentence in the entire project is that it serves as the hook – to get the reader to read the proposal and to begin to agree with the proposal. Basically the lead sentence compliments the proposal requestor as being a genius to ask for your proposal. Where possible try to use the exact words the client used to describe what he/she is looking for – including any buzz words or business jargon.

## Sample Background Statement

Senior Marketing Management at XXX industries believes that the company's sales organization strategy as currently constructed is suboptimal and seeks to evaluate and potentially implement a new organization strategy. (The who and what)

Over the past several years, XXX has lost market share to direct competitors even though the company's products and service levels have improved and are in some ways superior to competitors' products. Sales force turnover is increasing and anecdotal evidence from customer complaints suggest that the over-all performance of the sales force has declined in recent years. (The why)

The company seeks to implement the new strategy by the end of the third quarter of 20xx so the sales team will be optimized for the full year 20xx+1. (The reason to buy now)

## Your Unique Qualifications

For new clients or for projects where you anticipate you will be competing against other bidders I suggest a section on why you/your company is uniquely qualified to perform the assignment.

<u>Sample Unique Qualifications Statement</u>

We believe we are uniquely qualified to perform this important assignment for XXX Industries.

Joe Smow, the principal on this assignment, has designed sales forces for ten years and has revitalized sales forces for twenty of the largest sales forces in the xxxxxx industry. He has published articles in the two leading sales management trade magazines and his book "Winning in Sales" is currently a New York Times best seller.

Assisting Mr. Smow on this assignment will be:
- Fred Glutz who will conduct a number of interviews associated with this assignment. Mr. Glutz is the retired Vice President Sales at Leading Industries with over 30 years experience in sales and sales management.
- Sheila Jackson will design the performance model. Ms. Jackson has an MS in Financial Modeling and worked for a major financial consulting firm for ten years.

## Deliverables Statement titled "Assignment"

This sections tells the client exactly what they will get and in what sequence. In this section describe the methodology, assets you will employ and describe accurately exactly what the client will receive at the end of the assignment. As a rule of thumb don't overdo it here. I had a tendency to add too much in this section- always fearful of not getting an assignment – then regretted it when I actually had to do the work. Limit yourself to describing just enough work for you to get the assignment.

## **Professional Fee**

Here is a standard professional fee statement:

*The professional fee for the assignment is $150,000. The professional fee will be billed at 50% at project inception and 50% upon completion.*

*Travel and other direct expenses associated with the assignment will be billed as they are incurred.*

I always believe that a client should pay a hefty fee up-front. That way, the client has a dog in the fight – you essentially have a partner in the assignment and it solidifies the fact that you have a financial relationship.

The professional fee can be broken up into more than two segments and perhaps be tied to project phase completion or at various presentations during the assignment. In any case, I don't like a project inception fee any less than 30%.

If the client is nervous about travel expenses you can add. "Travel and other direct expenses associated with this assignment will not exceed $10,000" and/or "The client will authorize travel and other direct expenses before they are incurred." I don't like either of these.

## **Retainer professional fee should read:**

The monthly professional retainer fee is $20,000. The fee will be billed on the 20$^{th}$ day of the month before the retainer month. The professional fee for consulting days in excess of the number of consulting days listed in the Assignment section of this proposal is $3,000 per day and will be billed at the end of each retainer month.

## **Pricing**

Pricing is a critical success variable for an independent consultant and is frequently bungled by the novice Indy. The good news is that large consulting firms create the pricing umbrella and they charge a lot because they can and because of the large overhead they have in offices, receptionists, administrative assistants and huge partner compensation. Clients don't expect the Indy fees to be as high as the big firms but the big firms do make consulting for the Indy a profitable business.

**Most rookie Indies charge too little for their services**, as they don't realize the pricing umbrella created by the biggies, and they are nervous about losing accounts. Also, pricing is an art that you learn from experience in your specific field of what the market will bear.

My experience is that I cried when I left money on the table by under pricing and got really good at it over time. My biggest regrets during my consulting career were under-pricing. Pay attention to the following tips:

- Avoid pricing by the hour or the day – try to price by the project. Remember that you are providing the client with something they need. If you price by the hour or the day the client will do the math of how much money you are making, and possibly compare it to what he/she is making. You cannot leverage your time by hiring subcontractors at a relatively lower fee. Also, it makes you seem like a prostitute who gets paid by the hour!
- Figure out the pricing authorization level of the potential client. If it is zero, don't waste your time. This is a very common fake out as many people will talk to you about consulting but don't have any budget or spending authorization.
- Let's say a potential client's spending authority is $20,000 – Try to bring your bid in at $19,500 plus out of pocket expenses. If your consulting fee will be around $50,000 break the fee into program phases – priced at $19,500 for phases one and two, and the remainder for phase three, etc. The key is that you don't want the client to need to have his/her boss sign off on your job – because the boss could say "no" and also, the client likes to feel like the good guy to say "yes" to your proposal.

- If you have a long term relationship with a client or plan to have one, you can afford to undercharge on some assignments where you will lose a little bit on one job and can make it up on the next job. I have been known to say to a client "I am not making any money on this one but I know you need it so I will price it especially for you" - a great way to create long term client goodwill and client retention. I remember once, my client was on sick leave and his stand- in worked me on price just to show how tough he was. I pretended that he was the tough stud he thought he was and took the lower price because I knew I could make it up on my next assignment. Ironically, when he needed some work from me a year later, I stuck it to him on price.

- **Never, ever give away free advice!** Free consulting is worth what you pay for it! Clients will ask for freebies. Always answer, "let me prepare a proposal on that." I guess I am a little harsh here, so there may be some time you need to give a freebie – but seriously avoid the temptation. The temptation is very strong as someone asking you for advice is a big ego booster. Remember the pricing philosophy of psychotherapists is that if you don't feel the pricing pain, you won't take the advice. **Giving away freebies is one of the rookie Indy's biggest mistakes!**

- If a client calls you for free advice, try to convert the client to a "monthly retainer" at a price for him/her to call you when they want. I also liked retainers because it was a great opportunity to develop a strong relationship with the client on a professional and personal basis and to probe for future assignments.

## Expenses

The rule of thumb when you are pricing a project on a professional fee plus direct out of pocket expenses is that you should match the travel style of your client. For example, if your client stays at Day's Inn, you stay at Day's Inn. It the client stays at Hyatt, you stay at Hyatt. The lesson here is: don't outclass your client. The reason for this is that most clients will personalize your expenses and there is a chance a "green eyeshade" type at the company will say something about your rich living. Rarely, I would stay in a fancier hotel than my client, for example when I would stay in New York. In that case I would pay the difference of the bill myself and note that in the expense report.

Here are some other pointers.

1. Always rent a full sized car. Why? Because you will probably be driving in an area you are not accustomed- more metal means a better chance of survival. The bigger car is only a few bucks a day more than a smaller car. I got in an argument over this with a guy I was contracting for, who finally listened to me on this. He got in an accident and survived driving the full sized car.

2. Don't let the tail wag the dog on frequent flyer/frequent stayer programs. For example, don't drive a ½ hour from the airport to stay at your "points" hotel. Fly direct rather than earn two legs on your "points" airline. Do what's best for you and the client rather than max points. The rule of thumb is that the selection of hotels, flights and airlines should be based on "all things being reasonably equal."

3. Every company has its own quirks about expense categories. Some emphasize saving money on airlines while others focus on meals and entertainment. Get to know what the hot buttons are at each of your clients and try to max savings on those categories. On your expense report, note the savings. For example: "saved the client $400 by flying two legs rather than non-stop."

4. I tried to break even on expenses – meaning that I probably forgot a few expenses I didn't charge the client and I charged a breakfast I never ate. Do not cheat on expenses on the big stuff.

5. It is up to your conscience and your need for money if you are traveling for two clients at the same time and bill them each for the travel. In this situation, I always split the bill between the

clients and pointed out to the client what a hero I was to only bill them half of the travel expense.

6. Always submit professionally prepared expense reports – I used the program <u>Expensable</u> – but I am sure there are others. And attach receipts. Explain all entertainment expenses. If you have a taste for the grape/bourbon, eat the big bar tab - don't add it to the dinner bill. Make sure your entertainment expenses are not related to strip clubs, etc. unless you are consulting in that industry.

7. Generally, if you travel a lot, first class is a great benefit. But make sure you pay for the upgrade, not the client. Here is the exception: if you can get away with it, in your proposal you should state something like "for air travel in excess of 5 hours, consultants will fly business class on three classes of service flights and first class on two classes of service flights." If you are traveling with a client, always fly in the same level of service – not a good idea if you are in first class and the client is in coach!

## **Collections**

- Clients are notoriously slow payers – "invoice stuck to the in-basket tray" or simply, Accounts Payable is slow to pay. Accounts Payable at many company pay invoices in this order:
    1. Discounts for early pay – the traditional 2/10/net 30

    2. Penalties for late pay – "2% interest per month for all outstanding balances"

    3. Large suppliers of key product ingredients

    4. Smaller companies with low leverage – that's you!

The only solution is to call/contact the client and ask/beg for the money – the only tool is guilt. "Gee, I need the project inception money to pay my subcontractors" or "perhaps the invoice got stuck or misplaced at Accounts Payable, could you help me out here?"

- You could get "stiffed" by a client – not paid for the work performed. It is rare, as it happened to me only three times in over 30 years. In each case it was because the client believed I didn't deliver on the promised work or they didn't agree with the findings of my report. It is one of the reasons I believe in a hefty project inception fee. In each of these situations I ate the loss rather than "pissing in the well." If you have a great relationship with the boss of the client it might be worth making a case to the boss that you deserve the money.
- Cheated by contractors/"partners"

I was never cheated by a contractor for short term relationships but I was almost always cheated (in some cases substantially) by contractors in long term relationships, particularly in a shared percent of billings arrangement. I think it was usually that familiarity breeds contempt or the fact that they saw that I was entirely dependent upon them or they just thought they could get away with it.

You have limited recourse except legal action. Cheating by contractors is one of the strong arguments for keeping your relationships with a contractor relatively short and not depending on a single contractor for most or all of your revenue.

---

## **<u>Fee Negotiation</u>**

At some time you might need to negotiate a fee, particularly a retainer or a particularly large fee. I am a big fan of good cop, bad cop. Why? Although it seems like an old tired trick, it almost always works and even the best and brightest never recognize it. You, the Indy, should always be the good cop – "gee, I just want to help." The bad cop can be another person – a subcontractor to you, for example, or perhaps another person at the client who really needs you. If you use a subcontractor, you need to practice and or rehearse. I am a particularly good bad cop – I am naturally unlikeable and I love to act the part of bad cop. I was once in a negotiation on a retainer where I was the bad cop – I earned us an incremental $200,000 for a year retainer. The so called genius client mentioned to the Indy I was subbing for what a great guy the Indy was in the negotiations and what an asshole I was. So the Indy ended up the client's "hero" and I ended up with ½ the $200,000! By the way, it is easy to be a good cop but contrary to nature to be a bad cop – make sure the bad cop never slips into becoming a good cop. When you really get good at it, you and the bad cop can create an argument in front of the client. It is particularly effective for you to "admonish" the bad cop in front of the client.

In the absence of a bad cop I used "phantom" bad cops – a spend-aholic spouse, greedy subcontractors or suppliers, the IRS, other clients who were unreasonably demanding my time - you name it. I could really dramatize how bad the bad cops were – but of course I was the guy who just wanted to make a deal. When I retired, I brought my wife on the last business trip to meet my long term clients, and weren't they surprised when they realized she wasn't the mean spirited, big spender I had portrayed for ten years!

Also, I believe that at the end of negotiations it is important for you, the good cop, to give a little back. For example give back a few thou or add in a small consulting piece for free – even if the client was screwed in the negotiations, it makes them feel that they won in the end and it reinforces the notion that you are a really generous person.

I think the temptation for an Indy is to wimp out in negotiations because of the fear of losing the account. The rule of thumb is to not push for the last buck.

## Timetable

Here is a sample:

Given the importance of implementing a new come to market strategy for Acme, the timetable for this assignment is a "fast track" schedule.

The prospective timetable for this assignment is as follows

| Project Phase | Completion Date |
|---|---|
| Project Approval/Inception | |
| Phase One – Interviews completed | |
| Phase Two – Ideation session | |
| Phase Three – Plan Draft Completed | |
| Phase Four – Strategy Completed | |

I will call you to coordinate calendars to fix exact timetable dates.

## The Closer

In a letter format proposal, the closer should tie to the opening sentence – thus closing the proposal loop.

I prefer a proposal in a letter format rather than a proposal with a cover letter because the cover letter can become separated from the proposal and the cover and is a slight disconnect for the reader and does not lead the reader completely through the sell.

In a letter proposal, the lead sentence would read:

This letter is a proposal for Ace Consulting to assist the Acme Company in designing a new come to market strategy which will serve as the cornerstone for the company to increase its market share in the widget industry over the next five years.

The closer sentence would read:

I look forward to assisting Acme in transforming its come to market strategy and will call you early next week to get started and coordinate key milestone dates with you.

Very truly yours,

## **Verbal Proposals**

Sometimes a client may give you an order over the telephone. In that case use the same format as a written proposal.

Your telephone call should sound something like this:

"So Madison, what you need is xxxx; I will provide you yyyy; I will use method zzzz and deliver it on qqqq date for rrrr price. Is this right?"

A verbal contact is ok, but harder to prove than a written one– so I like to follow up a phone call contract with snail/e-mail. What happens if your client gets fired while you are doing the work?

# The Wrap Up

All the "must dos" I have listed in this book suggest to the most casual reader that you should very honestly and seriously evaluate your current position and abilities before deciding to become an Indy.

Although I have offered a lot of advice, the reality is that each Indy will experience different specific circumstances that I didn't cover.

I have offered you the benefit of my experience, but you must use your own good judgment and assume all the risks if you decide to become an Indy.

Good luck and good hunting!

www.ingramcontent.com/pod-product-compliance
Lightning Source LLC
Chambersburg PA
CBHW051815170526
45167CB00005B/2024